Remember the Brotherhood

Remember the Brotherhood

Poems of Carter Lee Aldridge

CARTER LEE ALDRIDGE

Edited by
MATTHEW ROBB BROWN

RESOURCE *Publications* · Eugene, Oregon

REMEMBER THE BROTHERHOOD
Poems of Carter Lee Aldridge

Resource Publications
An Imprint of Wipf and Stock Publishers
199 W. 8th Ave., Suite 3
Eugene, OR 97401

www.wipfandstock.com

PAPERBACK ISBN: 978-1-6667-3776-9
HARDCOVER ISBN: 978-1-6667-9759-6
EBOOK ISBN: 978-1-6667-9760-2

03/02/22

To Carter Lee Aldridge:
with thanks for your friendship and for a load
of delightful writings, artworks and wisdom.

And to Kay Elizabeth Brown
my friend and wife
for all these years of love and encouragement.

Do poets pray for each other?
Do poets pray for each other
In the shade or in the sun?
I know that light lies on their chests.
How can they absorb it?
Pray for me, Green Yankee poet
Of Antietam Creek.

—CARTER LEE ALDRIDGE

Appendix

Introduction

CARTER LEE ALDRIDGE WAS a friend of mine, a poet and artist with whom I had an ongoing relationship from 1973 until his passing in 1990. We met at Saginaw Valley College (Now Saginaw Valley State University), and shared what began as a friendship in our home town of Midland, Michigan (our family homes were within walking distance), which went on to be an extended correspondence after Carter moved, with most of his family, to Marietta, Georgia—to escape what they thought then to be dire future consequences of the energy crisis of the Nineteen Seventies. During all of this time, Carter and I shared literary and artistic works as well as news of events in each others' lives, and other ruminations.

I made a collection of the letters, poems, and linoleum block prints that Carter gave or sent to me during those years, as well as rare small-press publications in which our work appeared. From that collection, this book has been drawn.

What were originally poems have been retained in the form in which Carter or (sometimes) I wrote them. The prose letters, which tended at times to ramble, I have edited using the method known as "found poetry."

The book is intended to be, first, a good collection of poetry—and after that, a way of preserving and making available, in a readable format, Carter's work, which might otherwise be lost. For this reason, Carter's work predominates here, and I consider it a reasonable act of friendship to publish it.

I have a couple of copies of a book I created called The Carter Papers, which also exists as a file on my computer and, last time I checked, at Lulu.com, who printed the books. There is also, among my effects, an artist's backpack containing the original writings and letters from which that collection and this have been assembled, as well as the lino prints Carter created that are in my possession. Should those papers be preserved after my death, they may provide further material for study to anyone who might be interested. Should this take place, I give my apologies to the reader for the lack of proper organization and dates in the file. This exchange took place between 1973–1989 or so and can be placed in historical context accordingly.

While Carter expressed a certain reticence about his work, and perhaps would have been against its publication during his lifetime, it seems fitting now to make these works, many of which show a genuine and musical lyricism, and portray a unique person whom I think should not be forgotten, available to readers. Therefore, in the interest of friendship, I take this liberty, for the sake of those who might be as inspired as I have been by this interesting man and his work.

Acknowledgments

WHILE CARTER HIMSELF, ("NEXT to of course God") deserves first place in these acknowledgments, having supplied the lion's share of the contents of this book, I wish to include all kinds of other figures who inspired our poetry, our discussions, etc. Important among these are Gerard Manley Hopkins, Walt Whitman, Vincent Van Gogh, Erik Satie (performed by pianist Aldo Ciccolini), Claude Debussy (filtered through Isao Tomita's electronic performances on the album *Snowflakes Are Dancing*), Emily Dickinson, Thomas Merton, and so many more.

Philip Jesse Silva deserves mention for having edited a limited edition chapbook, *Your Own Poets*, in which both Carter's and my poems appeared.

Then there are teachers, including Marjorie Roberts, senior English teacher to both of us at different times at Midland High School, and Dr. Raymond Tyner at Saginaw Valley State University, whom we also had instructing us at different times, and who published our work in his literary magazine, *Green River Review*.

I could, of course, go on—but I would never be able to include everybody who influenced or helped us in any way.

So, I will conclude these acknowledgments with my friend and wife, Kay Elizabeth Brown, who has been a very appreciative reader of Carter's work, and has given me much encouragement and advice. I remember how, after we were married in 1982, Carter would always address both of us in his letters, even though he never had a chance to meet Kay.

—Matthew Robb Brown
Feast of Sts. Isaac and Ephrem of Syria
January 28, 2022.

PART ONE

Carter's Original Poems

DAWN

by Carter Lee Aldridge

Dawn,
Amber refraction along the heart,
Crystal autumn.
Frog on the road in spring
Like a leaf flapping over in the wind,
Seasons in a song, the old world,
Wells with butter cups and violets,
Mushrooms that paint themselves in
With deft strokes overnight—
For all things spare and simple, Lord,
Thanks be to thee.

HOLY, HOLY, HOLY

by Carter Lee Aldridge

I stood in the wind-rhythmed field,
Alone and full of circles;
I blessed the Sun with an apple
In my hand; forever supple, forever,
Are the Kansas-curtains of wheat blowing
That soothe away all my madness
With an inexorable repetition . . .
Holy, Holy, Holy . . . .

THE HUMBLE RAIN

by Carter Lee Aldridge

The humble rain
Falls in the lonely gutters . . .
How it conforms
To everything!
A leaf lies draped
Over a curb
In bland surrender.
So patient and submissive it is!
It condones every level.
Seeps and seeks the crevice,
Flows underground,
Emerges in the leafy wood,
Underguise of minerals,
Perpetrator of quiet rot,
The fumes of it coming forth
From the squelched wood.
[Copied into notebook in 1974]

[HUMBLE RAIN, ALTERNATIVE OR ORIGINAL VERSION]

by Carter

A leaf lies draped over a curb
In bland surrender.
Humble is the rain,
For it conforms to everything,
Seeks the gutter
At its own cost,
Surrenders to the drain,
Takes every hue,
And uses every crevice
As its home.

HUMBLE RAIN, ANOTHER VERSION

The humble rain falls
Into the lonely gutters . . .
How passive and receiving
It is to everything!
A leaf lies draped
Over a curb in bland surrender.
And I too am patient
In the patient rain—
We are of one mien.
It seeps and seeks the crevice
As its only home,
Conforms to everything
And condones every level.

HUMBLE RAIN, YET ANOTHER VERSION

The humble rain
Falls in the lonely gutters . . .
How it conforms
To everything!
A leaf lies draped
Over a curb
In bland surrender.
So patient and submissive it is!
It condones every level.
Seeps and seeks the crevice,
Flows underground,
Emerges in the leafy wood . . .
Underguise of minerals,
Rich soaker of wood,
Perpetrator of quiet rot,
The fumes of it coming forth
From squelched wood.

POEM BY CARTER LEE ALDRIDGE

[copied into notebook, 1974]

I ran, and like the
    crest of a wave,
        falling,

I tumbled under
    my motion

And lay there, fallow
    like a field

In my thoughts and
    free.

Fresh breezes came over
    me and lulled me

And the world seemed to
    spin.

I got up, Lord:

I'm walking now—

"Woe to him

Who sets his hand to the
    plow

And then turns back."

I CRAVE MY GOD

by Carter Lee Aldridge

(Late summer, 1972)

I crave my God
With a secret craving
That sets the world aslant for me.
He is that level something
That I would know.
How much better than I am
Are you, sweet Lord,
Prayer of my adolescence
And answer to that agony as well.
Be my luck in time of sorrow.
I love you better than you know.
I love you better
Than I have let you know.

RIDE TO CENTER

by Carter Lee Aldridge

There will be a true time for ardor to see.
A fine and filial comet, as if wanting to adore,
Faithfully streaked back to bathe itself
In the rewards of the sun's rays, and may,
Who knows? Have lilted in a peaceful, perfectly
          optical curve
Through our window on space as we slept . . .
(droopy-eyed, we say we saw a smudge . . .)
We felt the momentary drama; it presaged to us . . .
We heard an Announcer fading in, like this:
"Others say they saw a vision of a split triangle
Unwrap itself, spin and scintillate,
Smoothing inward to the scientific nudge,
Huge bulge of the terrific sun-border . . ."

RESTING WITHIN A STONY NOOK

by Carter Lee Aldridge

On market night, I enter the candlelit church above
The street, carrying no thought but
The Bible resting in a stony nook;
Old, golden with lacquer, and glued,
Is the Book—I orient myself to its
Retrospects—unfasten the leathern hasps,
Hearing weathers of grace, and harps—
There in Job I learn
The earthenware I am, the housed worms.
In Proverbs I learn the hooks of vital lure
That attract me, and am warned.
Down again I have to go, to the street-common
Level; market night is dust-thick, and I
Must eat of that vitality, seeing the beggar boy,
Who sells fish and luck. Now swings
The full censer of the hung bauble moon
In our warm skies; wondrous industry's vapours cloud,
And move, like this crowd,
Amid the massed lofty heads of palmettos, amid
Traders of families, and tinkling of brass.

RESTING WITHIN A STONY NOOK [VERSION 2]

by Carter Lee Aldridge

On market night, I enter the candlelit church above
The street, carrying no thought but
The Bible resting in a stony nook;
Old, golden with lacquer, and glued,
Is the Book—I orient myself to its
Retrospects—unfasten the leathern hasps,
Hearing weathers of grace, and harps—
There in Job I learn
The earthenware I am, the housed worms.
In Proverbs I learn the hooks of vital lure
That attract me, and am warned.
Down again I have to go, to the street-common
Level; market night is dust-thick, and I
Must eat of that vitality, seeing the beggar boy,
Who sells fish and luck. Now swings
The full censer of the hung bauble moon
In our warm skies; wondrous industry's vapours cloud,
And move, like this crowd,
Amid the massed lofty heads of palmettos, amid
Traders of families, and tinkling of brass . . .
Still I am comforted
By the quiet of one stony nook,
And the stone-cupped oil lamp
Providing light on the One God's Book.

Carter Lee Aldridge / revised version / September 16, 1977

A POEM IN ORDINARY TIME

by Carter Lee Aldridge

I. Your Living Room, Like a Hotel

I've taken off the shoes
Of my indifference, padding now
With foot-feeling
The carpets of your patient luxury . . .
Such svelte expanses affront
That last soul I bore, being
Nearly as clean, as spare, as
It was . . . Sufficiency wants to
Define itself here. Here stop,
Look upon the shelf, where a
Bottle of pills states, beside
the inscription of a globe,
'Quiet World', a sleep helper . . .
It's all so unobtrusive, so
Self-effacing, material to ethereal . . .

II. Stopped to Hear Bells

Harmonics of the heart in Fall
Taught me how to listen
To quelling of my heart by bells,
Bells now tintinnabulated lightly
By a tapping elder branch. I've
Stopped here by the woods,
Stilled the humming of my wheels,
And counterweights and lifters—
All resting . . . No time to go farther,

For an inner argosy has begun.
What Jason has escaped with
All the randy rabble of my thoughts?

III. A Day of Little Things

It's 'Ordinary Time' in churches again;
Ordination has begun. I want to learn
The parable of daily life, grooving-in
The pattern deeply. I want to relate
To my trees: Christ again. (I hugged
One of them in Kentucky, mid-travel).
I opened a boxed memory: my cowries
Still crouch together, a pretty crowd . . .
In the library, I search the stacks
For a pressed flower . . .
Is it time to bring forth
The now-feathered bird of imagination,
And feature it toward the north?

IV. Aesthetics of Cold Weather

North reached into me, with fingerlets
Of ice, refreshed me with snaps of
Alertness; locket by locket, North
Searched her memory of
Being a Child of the North, and clasped
Her ring with cold. I fingered the eel
Of thoughts going far away: it was
Cold, fast, considerate of distance . . .
Snows came, and were like
A wall trying to form . . . And the poet said,
'Ah! Where are the snows of yesteryear?'
He meant beautiful young women . . .

V. In the Schook Bar, 1973

In a quickened time, the quick sang
To the dead, in a bar
On peanut night (throwing the shells
On the wooden floor freely . . .)
How my feet moved, and the squashed shells
Said, as they collapsed, 'Quick! quick!'

VI. In the Woods, 1963

One time a boy entered the woods
And saw a luna-moth on a stone . . .
The moth was heart-green, and
He amply sharpened a stick, and
Impaled the thing for display—and
All the trees in the world fell down . . .

VII. Driving Somewhere, Alone

My name must go before me as a prow,
Breaching waves . . . Virile road-expanses
And wind, are boldly fronted by
My car window; I sit calm before
Dials, spirit-indicators of
Busy normalcy, seated again in
An auditorium of fierce concise intent . . .

VIII. In the Library

A quiet-world, thought-world library,
Where no raucous rhythm-sections
Thrum with power, but where I read
A rainy-day poem; slanting, sideways,
All awry. Tension tries to slide in,
Insinuate itself between
The poem and me. The poem
Glows in warning . . . I feel

A prayer arise: 'Oh God, let me
Interview a child today . . . '

IX. In Pennsylvania Woods, 1962

Our tree we sat on, bent by Indians
Long ago, sits sidelong in the air:
We say—'Let's go out and sit and talk
In the air on the Old Leaner . . . '
A spirit speaks, from boles of trees:
"I offered the land to you,
My sons and daughters, by laying
Fish before you, upon it: this
Fish dedicates the hill for you.
Take the hill. And so, my empty
Cup, too, offers you fullness to fill . . .
Eglantine, you called the vine . . .
But the trees, when they harp
And sough together, echo a surer
Set of words: Elegant Vine, the
Vision to within—and
A horse heard in the wind . . ."

["A Poem In Ordinary Time," written late 1970's according to note; Carter
gave it to me in typescript form. I remember this being around 1977 when
Carter, Phil and I published *Your Own Poets*.—MB]

DEAR FRIEND

by Carter Lee Aldridge

"You look a lot less,
They would say, today;
Some one hundred fifty pounds,
Going some months now;
Awhile afore, and you were
One-hundred and eighty.
(He looked like Hopkins' brindled cow.)
Oh, for clothes that don't fit,
And ancient dears, locked in place
By photographs, the rummage
I throw to find the correct word . . .
Here's running, friend, to find you;
You are like me, some,
And we both look
For that inestimable sum of our work.

POEM FOR JOURNAL, A PRELUDE

by Carter Lee Aldridge

The verdict was, you were
Lovely in your youth . . .
Now bend to the babbles
And charts of love's course:
Your heart precedes you . . .
Item #1 is that where
Love has existed, everything
Is marked . . . Item #2
Is that, under pressures of
Suffering, the soul becomes
As a diamond. Write these
In your Book of Hours . . . On the
Title page, write: "Lumen Hilare,"
Or—the Light of Laughter . . .
This has seemed as The Saviour,
When, unnoticed, it stood
Somewhere you needed to go,
And paved the way to go there . . .
Now, be deep-seated in your chair,
Feeling like the Sultan of Sit,
And let your patience discover your guest again.

POEM FOR THE SPRING LADY; OR, POETIC DIALOGUE

by Carter Lee Aldridge

Poet speaks:
"Wall, why do you protect me?
Who am I? Why are you always
At my side?"

Answer:
"I block off for now
That part of the Glory
You cannot bear: look
The other way . . ."

Poet speaks again:
"I look the other way,
And my love loves a grief
That is pure; I see her
Standing in the spring pools,
Bare feet and mullein-flavored
Skirt . . . There is a love that
Loves a grief that is pure,
Oh my God . . ."

"Water has been on my mind
All day—that is outside,
In pools, by the breadcrumb
Snow, in little maddened creeks,
Where crawdaddies live, as if
Only for this delight: that they
Dart about at your magic touch . . ."

"The birds have their lives
Under a heaven of trees;
And I have had mine
In the waters of ease . . ."

SCHOOL BEGINS WEDNESDAY

by Carter Lee Aldridge

Waiting for prayers in August,
Prayers of the heart's inquest,
And ones of schools coming together
Again, the opening of the old scrolls;
I walk through picture-puzzle leaves
Of oak, but can't stop now to try
To make them fit; the chant of the strength
Of a northern people goes through
My head: "oak and hickory, oak and hickory . . ."
Always . . .

Food only tastes so good
When the air has such a fine edge, when
The churlish cold is hurrying;
And the cheer kept so well, even by
Animals adept in the cold, as the fire leaps
A whisper even beyond the snow . . .

POEM: WORKSHOP

by Carter Lee Aldridge

[Carter's notes: "Sent to *Commonweal* on Sept. 15, 1977."
and, "edited by Matthew Brown"]

The sifting of my own joy
Has produced high capital,
As by sifting the iron scrap
The forger grasps the best element.
The blows by a sound mind,
But one too strange in its *hauteur*,
Seemed too strong, almost, though
The anvils were of such thick tang,
Density of thought that rang true . . .
But there was more delicate work,
There, rare things,
Like the bronze chimes that rankled
In your doorway when a blustery wind,
Myself, blew in. A gentler contemplation
Unwinds, like butterfly nets releasing
Hordes, in a color-argosy; as the name "Jesus,"
Light as a bird, flies in through the hat
Of my house, a light chiming
Begins, growing, growing . . . .

JESUS

by Carter Lee Aldridge

On into distances of vista, destiny,
Train whistle, bird call,
Or wind's deep measure of sound,
In blizzards, in time's wrecks
And in the eternal backyards of life
Where the litter of our life is stored
(Or in basements, where we collect
Our hours in tangible referents
Of time)
I see him lead me.

POETIC MINIATURES AND FRAGMENTS

by Carter Lee Aldridge

1
The rose of years
Has intercepted time.
Shards of silence
Interpenetrating
Now coalesce
To form a whole.

2
The shape of my dying is vast.
You great summonings of cloud,
Pray me new soft lands.

3
Do poets pray for each other?
Do poets pray for each other
In the shade or in the sun?
I know that light lies on their chests.
How can they absorb it?
Pray for me, Green Yankee poet
Of Antietam Creek.

4
Deep in Ohio there is a television
That winks at day,
Being in shadow of a grandmother's past,
Using to come on
Quietly while it rains . . .

It looks like summer's words are over.

5

Oh sheepish twilight,
Come from behind
Those trees.

6

The young beech whispers to the forest,
'Misty flowers I have seen.'

7

Could there be strings plucked
For every leaf-sound slight
Upon the water or the ground
What music would they make?

8

Spider Web

Reaching through elements of time,
This solemn filament is seen, whose orb,
When projected, forms the bias of things.

9

The strategy was flame,
And all ardor concurred;
In the night the Allah
Of the burgundy whisperers
Was stirred.

10

Little Song

She was on the green,
And the green was deepening,
Her satin shimmering . . . .
The water was advancing,
But she was on the green,
And the green was deepening.

11

Crying has revealed the elder tree.
Circle of laughter dropped clean into snow.

12

I have made a covenant with
My backyard: I shall sit there
As often as the birds pipe madly.

13

Prisms that focus heaven,
Music behind my iris,
Ruck-sack for stilly gems, have I,
To win this heaven on the sly.

14

Autumn Night

Chill me, oh night,
As stars are chilled,
That tremblesome I
May be more spry
To taste the autumn nectar . . .

15

Photographer

I caught mountains in the clouds
And gave them embrace.
But closer was the river
That the mountain shed.

A LOVE POEM FOR SOMEONE POSSIBLE

by Carter Lee Aldridge

Sometimes, dear, in grace I miss you.
Sometimes, while reading Walt Whitman,
I want to read you into my Whitman—
And so I do . . .
Who are you, that I will love, except
A concatenation of the many loves
I have already loved?
Will you with your eyes
Be shaping me into you, as I now
Shape you into me?
I have your mercy in my hands,
Because you have put it there
With a touch . . . Have you my mercy in yours, too?
While reading these old lines
Of the venerable Whitman, I feel
The old ability coming back
To bear the lines that nerve me to joy
Without wincing under the intensity,
Without running from sublime pressures of love . . .
Once again I take the test of this passion.
I want to bring all I have,
And all I am into you; I want the poems
I have read with my soul as my intent:
Let me tell you of, utterly quashed
And quelled, a love great enough to shout about . . .

IT'S QUIET HERE

by Carter Lee Aldridge

It's very quiet here. I wrote a poem today
which was inspired by a song. Here it is—

The wind blows toward me,
And leaning into it, I say,
Stardrops in clusters,
Raiments in wind;
Rain on the dust,
And harmony in air,

For all these things so fair,
The things of pity
Will grow strangely dear,
There in the half-light,
Inviting speculation.

* * *

I'm about to write a poem;
it's sort of like hatching an egg
—it's a better egg when mature.
So sometimes I wait longer.

* * *

I know that my spirit is extremely intelligent
—I mean apart from my mind.

* * *

I went to church for the first time
in a long time this last Sunday.
I hope I will keep it up in the Sundays to come.

(FOR MATTHEW)

by Carter Lee Aldridge

March 6, 1977

Cold rain makes me forget who I am.
"Rememberer of histories,"
"Spewer of theorems," "Listener to wind-symphonies,"
"Sad logician," "Always frank, never merry,"
I have gone down the lists
To only this, the rain's cold strategems.

"Catch me coldly
In silly old buckets,
Crumpled in like old men . . ." says rain
To me, and laughs on, and a train
Whistle-silvers down the night—
As if a harp, or flute, no whistle,
    had vibrated
As thistle by wind will hum—
Tell me what it's like to be alone, without money,
In the night, on the great faith-trestle.

I am gone down to cold rememberings,
And the mist is my memory, gold-mist,
And the puddles are my playthings.

ISLANDS, AND BEYOND

by Carter Lee Aldridge

The sun reached ripened, amber fire,
Glinting off the islands
Of my soul's own true imagining,
Of moments spent with God . . .
On the map, they are like brethren—
And now they are at work silently,
And at nightfall call to each other
For cheer.
Who is the lonely outlier, in supplication?
Let each man, before God, have entirely his own
Shore . . . Because Jesus is for us, two
Watchers on distant islands,
Become one longing in their prayer,
And reach one resonant accord.

THE CHANTING OF THE TRAIN

by Carter Lee Aldridge

The train goes by every night
To remind me of you, O Lord;
To remind me of my longing for you—
For the train is long, and is longing away,
    with a trailing horn,
        bending, leading away,
Now faintly (O faintly, but clearly still I hear
    thy call! My mind's ear is already
    following thee).
Thou hast others to go to, as the train;
I love them too in Thee—haste away
    to my brethren, thy horn sounding clear—
I follow this sweet voice . . .
But you have passed by here close, to remind me once again . . .

(OLDER POEM)

by Carter Lee Aldridge

Daily on the radio I hear them calling—
The great minstrelsy
Calling all the merry people to the dance—
Calling all the world to trance—
Love is a word like any other word:
Transposed, revealed, rejected,
Or trammeled in the soundwave paradise
Of forty airings of a song . . .

POEM ALREADY IN PROGRESS WHEN YOU CAME

by Carter Lee Aldridge

And he shall announce in the grave
That the very laughter
Which served to reprove him
Is now turned back
To thwart his fledgling's purpose;
His turn to reprove.
Fastidiousness, years of remorse,
Objects set up for eyes to woo
As if their stability were romance
With reality when contemplated,
But in fixity of gaze idolized—
These things will be open to view
And sterile objects will no longer do.
But that longing upward glance
He will not revile, when you,
Judging by distance, figured
On eternity as a ride just begun,
Discoveries yet to come.

ADVERTISEMENT

by Carter Lee Aldridge

When my heart tries
At their mountains,
All my heart's ties
Seethe to fly away into bliss . . .
Strange, for I've missed this,
Yet know, just as sure,
Someday I'll go to them,
WITH AN ARGOS CAMERA.

YET YOU CALL US WRITERS

by Carter Lee Aldridge

We like to be awake at night,
To watch the WORLD, our planet,
    from our windows and our
    high parapets, balconies, and spires:
Hidden in recesses in the hilly woods,
Thick woods with mist; you know Where!
Mist within and everywhere, except:
    the inner circle of our
Castle, where,
    instead of deep mist and SHADE,
arises a dome high and of Clear
    LIGHT!
        of COURSE!
Yet, you call us vampires. You
    entered that dome by mistake;
We
    have been deliberate
            about
    going
            in and out
    of it
        for a Lo-o-o-ng Time!
We are writers . . .

POSTCARD

by Carter Lee Aldridge

Dear Samoset,
Arrived at the towers—
Am enjoying the lucrid distance,
The old dictionary,
Dim crockery corners—
Am whisking the light away
In Camelot, where we ran together . . .
Dave sends his wishes . . .
Yours truly,
    with mayhem,
        Supposititious—
P.S. Enjoyed your sullied,
    hangdog expression
    at our last meeting . . . .

A saying I recall hearing
more than once from Carter:

"Is there a fillip of hope for a trollop?"

This was not meant to be offensive but
is an example of the word-play we
sometimes engaged in.—M.B.

FISHER OF SOULS

by Carter Lee Aldridge

He went fishing, released
For the suspicions of purple,
From the constrictions of day,
And the heart's delay—
Pole in hand, and walking—
The smooth stones slid,
The bole
Of the rod dipped, as if to point where—
And then slid forth gurgling
From purple shadows ambulating
Across the easy water
A most secret fish (no shallow thing).
With sensitive nets
He scuttled
The prize, and prized his adventure
In his eye . . ."This thing
Is most sleek and slippery of all
Those things that are gone to hide
In dignified deeps, in shallows,
In shoals, or in the reeds—
Where even little Moses hid . . ."
Laughter came from the raucous-wild swallows
Busy in the pawnshop
Of husk and seed,
And he said: "And yet this thing
Does not show an air of regret,
But eagerly slaps my palms . . ."
"Let me now lay the shank aside,
And take thought for the Bible,
Even as shadows secrete
The Land of Lost Thought . . ."

He read, and as He got up, prophesied:
"Now mercy will take a tent,
And, penurious of cares,
Wander where it will, to many."

Touch will sing to touch,
And hills will signal hills . . ."

[One of the few poems bearing a date, this is dated October 6, 1977. I was considering this poem for possible publication, perhaps in *Your Own Poets,* which was published in the fall of that year.]

A "TIME-POEM"

by Carter Lee Aldridge

    The freckled grain
of bread.
    The good, good
sweat of summer . . .
    Grain, that
        cries
           in
               us
                    deep:
Oh! Sunset, at the Solstice!
Come: soon our Equinox:
    b a l a n c e
        r
        e
        s
        t
        s.
Once more the balance
Rests upon the ledger,
At our Autumn Equinox:
Once more.
    Winter
        soon:
            Solstice . . .

(A SUDDEN RAIN)

by Carter Lee Aldridge

A sudden rain . . .
It falls on the Mind
To replace the waters lost
From the freshness invested
In the body.
One lake, this body,
Subject to boredom's evaporation,
In flowing the word of God,
The word being supreme
When hypnosis has fallen away.
I love the rain,
It finds me in corners,
I touch it and it photographs
Me in its pools.

(THE APPLE OF CONTENTMENT)

by Carter Lee Aldridge

The apple of contentment has sat upon
My high inner window sill; it dropped
There from my girl-and-boy befriended hand.
I watch it now—it is as if years of window sills
Travel down in these ripples and these rills,
That like sighs, pool, tremble, tipple over the edge,
                      and escape.
To escape I am afraid.
The hails of your friendship, or prayer,
And the "all-accounting will be made"
I promised were, to me, like nails
To firm things with, but how they always seemed
To bend, then rankle, and mar the too-good surface.

Now driving them straight I true up the boards;
With these words I can aid; I drive them rivet-like, too,
Into God-forged faithfulness, or into the new deep
Pithy stuff of friendship . . .

Pastor Jack once said about being forgiven,
"Holes remain in the holy pine
When yet the long nails be removed."

"Pastor Jack," I said, "I am reproved."

I watch as the apple sits there, and I am wistful
To watch it shrink and wither, until
My sense of taste shall see me fit to eat it—
What until has sat so neat. Withered apple
Before me, be more holy-some meat.

[Carter polished this into "Waiting Onward" in *Your Own Poets.*]

POEM FOR THE RAIN-HECTIC ONE

by Carter Lee Aldridge

That diamantine beginning began,
On floors too hard
For the diamond to roll.
The jazz began to sing.
The operatic jewel began
To deliberate
In the opium capital of the world—
When withywindle got her cliff,
Off the North, the jewel-clef
Got off to the rain-world,
The seas in diamond and jazz!
Now my humble boulevard
Got her rain-umbrella
And her urn, her bravado touche,
And the scorch of the templar,
Who was the secret of the capitol, jazz.
Who was the arcane?
Who were rare, in the jungle-story?

[signed] Carter Lee Aldridge, Jr.
Midland, Michigan—
Fall, 1979

HAVING DRIVEN TO HILL CHURCH

by Carter Lee Aldridge

(a poem for Jesus)

1 The eyes of penury never forget
Those eyes uplifted importuning joy
For those in the morning lauds with them,
Though spread far and thin, His Body—
It seems especially suspicious
To doubt the treasure at hand, the
Involvular pleasure of the hilly land,
Rising, under a car's command!
At His Word, laughter: it will
Spill, when pains are done, into
The great grooves and gouges carved,
Reservoir enough. Ah! Canyon Grande,
Who mouthed you is far more vast!

2 Out in the garden, roaming muskily,
How the glory hurts! The rose, the tiara,
The music from within . . . The stars above,
like iron, to my loves, of tin . . . .
I, blank, and I am wincing:
How the glory hurts!

3 Quiet time: let illusions bear
The cross I could not
Completely bear
Myself: I am
At relief, and seven pm
But when I wake
          and rouse
Myself to duty,
          again,

May I remember the man visited
At his door by fear:
"I am all you could not face: today
I shall act it out
In your place."
Carter Lee Aldridge, 230 North Saginaw Road, Midland, Michigan 48640
[Handwritten comment: Here is a poem I've worked on lately—]

FOR THOSE GIRLS; A RETURN TO AUSTERITY

I.
I am homely in illusion, but I
Am being angeled to death
By the pert-eyed looks of
Demi-mondes like these, that
Pass me by. A magic tornado,
Love, has descended. Perhaps
There are ways of stealing a
Glance, to farther within that
Storm, if eyes are quick; perhaps
I can get around this glory
Unscathed. But no. the emotional
Miasma has included me, this time.
So, I'll play a piano, in keying up
To their wonders, plucking the
Ripe notes down from the air,
So gingerly. I'll stud the air
With them, bright and punctual.
II.
Then, suddenly, as the subtle
Yet huge awareness of Autumn Orion
Climbs to view, and I am going home
On some road royally lined with
Trees, and see the handsomeness
Of the house that grew out of her,
I stop: I am changed to strength
For her sake, charged to greaten,
In the lees of my falling wonder.
Orion, the Sign—that ruggedness
Wants the austerity of the single-eyed
Star, in the coldest morning.
White eternity roves in this snow,

Inflicting severities of Reason
Upon my coddled senses—once,
And for all. I'd like to measure
My relation to God—but how well
Can I bend or temper steel?

THE OUTDOOR HEARTH

by Carter Lee Aldridge

You are alone in time, Sir,
In the bonfire's lights;
The others are gone away
To banquets or the safe kiss . . .
Whole barns with rafters full
Of thoughts seem to emerge to you—
The fire is pleasant by
Relation to a present gloom.
Laughter seems to start up
When rain-spatters pounce,
Producing a hurried hiss . . .
You think of the one here lately,
And say: "In her lap sat propped
The beautiful girl herself,
Wrapped within wrap, and lap
Withinholding lap, forever, in love . . ."
And the land's own fine bosom rises,
Beautiful, and as rare of mood—
Heaving, without thunder,
Without a breath, that you
Could hope to hear . . .

POEM: FEAR OF NATURE AND ANTHROPOMORPHISMS

by Carter Lee Aldridge

Thought of a pulsing city
casts me into melancholy
at once, and terribly;
Thought of Mother Earth
casts me into melancholy
at once, and forcibly.
Oh no, it isn't true,
It isn't true, how can it be?
That blue tent, the sky,
with a shaft of amber
wants to have no sun
but shine by itself alone;
That heathered maze,
the earth, wants to be flat
and unwind itself forever,
and consist in itself alone.
Oh no, it isn't true,
It isn't true, how can it be?

With credit to Shakespeare I think for the phrase 'heathered maze' with an offhand reference to the Book of Revelation in which the New Jerusalem has no sunlight but gets its light from God. [typed comment by Carter]

Poems from the Chapbook,
Your Own Poets

[The following poems by Carter first appeared in *Your Own Poets*, a limited edition anthology of poetry by Christians, edited by Philip Jesse Silva. The two poems of mine from the anthology that I wish to have remembered will appear in a later book. Phil, Carter, and I had the book printed and we collated and stapled the copies ourselves in the basement of Phil's family home on East Ashman Street in Midland. It is a limited edition of 600 copies hand-numbered by Phil, copyright 1977 and published in the autumn of that year.]

OH TREASURED FIELD

by Carter Lee Aldridge

He stood in the curve of the awe
Of the Act, and believed; it was not belied.
He stood by the tacit fact
And brooded out his silence;
He stood in the altar-cave
And worshiped with a stance;
He straightened him up with a staff;

The limp flag of his life
Had no whiff of wind to play—
He brooded in the altar-cove
And embraced the Cherished;
Light-carving entrances revolved
As the world-hooded wish seemed
More than the books of Autumn had to say
Of the grief of the broken bread:
And he sang, "Oh treasured field . . ."

[Carter's note: ("remember the word-play of 'entranced' as you read
'entrances')

POEM FOR A MAN, BLACK, ABOUT FORTY

by Carter Lee Aldridge

There's a thing
I wanted to say to you,
But only you:
Your blackness is my shield.
Your blackness is my shield.

BE STILL AND WEAVE

by Carter Lee Aldridge

I have fairly resolved to go down
Below my house, in rough garments,
Into basements and cellar-grottoes
Of my mind and of my house,
That smell musty like old shoes,
Places a mushroom colony might swell
As in old piles of compost . . .
Sitting among the clumpy stuff of ages,
Burly, eccentrically squarish,
Surface-iridescent, whole heaps of it,
Worse than fish piled on docks,
I will heap up praises to Him,
Keep up praises to Him away
From shudders of the mantle-clock,
Though it kept time to His praise,
Too, I think. Times like this I wonder
About the dank mystery of misery
In winter . . . But I will hear a time,
After augury of clouds, when I'll be saying,
With the birds in codified praying
"It's time for elms and maples;
For seed-helixes, floating down to place,
Have in their scattering thrown
A lovely warp-and-woof pattern down
About the world; in our shoes we shift
Their auburned seeds and husks all day.
God so ordered summers green: "Be still
                    and weave."

WAITING ONWARD

by Carter Lee Aldridge

The apple of contentment has sat upon
My high inner window sill; it dropped
There from my girl-and-boy befriended hand.
I watch it now—it is as if years of window sills
Travel down in these rain-looped ripples and rills,
That like sighs, pool, tremble, tipple over the edge,
                                        and then escape.
To escape I am afraid.
The hails of your friendship, your prayer,
And the once all-accounting hour I promised were
Like nails—but how they always seemed to bend,
Rankle, and mar the too-good surface!
Now driving them stiff and final, I true up the boards at last;
Promises I urge to drive like rivets, rivet-fast,
Into God-forged faithfulness; hails of friendship
And facts of prayer I mend with; Good News accountings
Are good hardy three-penny nails to drive
Into the deep pithy beam-thrusts of our new friendship,
And our trusts . . .

I watch as the apple sits there, and seems almost
To shrink and wither as I watch, wistful until
My sense of taste shall see me fit to eat it—
What until has sat so neat.
Withered apple before me, be more holy-some meat.

OUR PETITE BUT VOLUMINOUS GARDENS

by Carter Lee Aldridge

The precious heart-nut has graced my health,
The heath where in Lamb's milk I was refreshed;
I am grown prolix with song as vine-scrawled bricks
With creepers, or as The Book with the strong nurture
Of His Word. Winds I have captured, winds that have
Escaped, have taught me the truth of another year,
Worlds apart: twelve years old I see myself again,
In the balmy sequestery of summer Bible-school; tender
Shoots of the palms of victory sprung up, and then
Fanned me in the air with breaths, scented only
Faintly, but with rumours vast and great: sweetwater
Rains came after our Eastertide Church, with wind,
And you turned to her, father, yes you said:
"It's just a grace-shower . . ." Teach me, I pray,
Thou Gardener, my florid nooks; let us be bravely
Lovely for Thee, Who art so great. I have made
This covenant with my backyard, that I will sit there
When the birds all sing madly (To Thee, Sir).

POEM: FOR MY RETREAT

by Carter

I see my room widening with suns,
In radiance of containment.
But containment is to be
A malicious word
To anyone who does not know
Wherewith he contains
That which is fortified here.
I know the instrument
O my containment; here it lies upon
The table. I call upon it, and it is
At my constant beck and call:
The rhythm of prayers of the saints,
Graceful rhythms of a Kempis in chapters . . .
Love lies valleyed with its rain,
And open to the snow. So
Doubt not that rooms will fill themselves:
Once will come a room that needs nothing.
Don't touch the mote in your eye, then;
Say: "The eye of the room is your eye now."

A HAND-MADE CHRISTMAS CARD

(with block print in black of a shepherd and angels)

No date

Holy God,
We praise Thy Name;
Holy God,
We adore Thee—

Bless you, Matthew & family
Your friend, Carter

POEM FOR GRANDFATHER AND GRANDMOTHER

by Carter L. Aldridge

God has risen in this world.
And He will rise in the next world.
And in every world. His great peace
Justified me
To work more deeply into my works,
And the gift was worth repeating to you.
Now, in the
Affection of our pleasant night heat,
It is "the old bed," I say; "the old bed . . ."
Made by stages more common than I ever was,
With the same familiar affection
With which I speak of an old patchwork quilt
Made by someone I loved very much,
I can say of Him now (I love Him)
"They could not keep the old boy down:
He rose up early, hale and hardy;
His eyes were bristling with purpose;
Lovely apothegms lanced off his tongue,
Eager to be spoken to a waiting world,
That it might in its turn remember
Something spoken long ago, around which
The myriad of lives took form, and which
Put magical sons around the tables,
Ready to resound and sing to our future
Their word and action and their fables . . ."

(LIND)

Lind, all the valley
Hears the candor
Of your cloying call,
Oversweet,
As you spread the sweet plums
Out to the sun.
Does the breeze catch your skirt,
And the sun bedapple your blouse
With even deeper orange
Than it relatively is inside?
Your window, then, you there
At your mirror,
And the span of these thoughts . . .
It's evening,
Spices to you, I wish . . .

The following selection of poems, which I dubbed "fantasy lyrics," are pieces written by Carter, which have in common that they allude to or set scenes in untold fantasy stories, more or less in the mold of Tolkien or C.S. Lewis. This really started in the early 1980's when Carter sent a letter which included a fair copy of "Poem" (for Kildarrow). The fantasy lyrics which I have written will appear elsewhere, since they mostly post-date the period covered in this collection.

POEM (KILDARROW)

by Carter Lee Aldridge

[Hand-printed fair copy]
(Circa 1984)

The secret sorrows of Sirenon
Were of covenant none;
None but Kildarrow could master them,
And he died by the gold-tipped arrow.

Lately the duvenant* witches cry
And cast their hemp on the barrow;
None but Kildarrow could oppose them,
But he died by the gold-tipped arrow.

Close and cling so tight to the secret tree
That grows in County Midlothian;
For Midlothian is in the heart, as they say—
And Kildarrow is in the ocean.

* coined word in context [Carter's note.]

SIRENON'S PRAISE BY CARTER LEE ALDRIDGE

[Hand-written, enclosed in a letter dated February 8, 1987.]

When Lord Sirenon was twenty-one
He saw a sword thrust through the sun;
Then Niamith his queen ran up unto the boundary roses
And stood in a design of quandary aces—
Only aces! and merely aces!
A mystical fawn of Altaris their sun
Strayed across her revenant path, rondured
By the fallwood and heated by the breath of flowers!
So he laid on its neck for to wear
A stone crucifix. Such were this pair,
In typical days under the sun.
Their summer was called Falgium.
Their winter was called Migrail.
The number of their days together
Was twenty-three hundred and one.

GRAND MASTER STORMWISE

by Carter Lee Aldridge

[Undated typescript or carbon copy.
I received it not too long after the first Sirenon poem.]

What is this that burns, sears,
                    crackles through the Fold?
Tongues of indignation that now lash
                    and scatter off at
Caught truths in caught throats . . .
"Another world's scar heals that of this . . ."
        Barbed, bold spears of lightning thrash out
                            over the Fold,
        hasting to their garments of righteousness;
They wring and wrestle out their awe over all
                        fair Midlothian—
        Addis Ababa too calls out, and *softly*, "Come in here,
                            pray awhile."
Yet through throat's deep,
                    calls go out to another deep—
        "For deep shall call out unto deep, in that day . . ."

One of the lightning rods alone has stood,
                    lashed itself onto
        the spear multifold, and ridden it down to earth—
Who could have riddled it? That One, whose House we yesterday
        did not see, stood perfectly still to take it all in—
The Wise One's shelving, surging,
                    delving lightnings?

Rod of Jesse, flowering . . . (Do you see, now, awesome canopies
        that sweep down upon it?)
Say, do you see Jesus? "Whose House," we wondered, "could that be?"

LOGRAIRE

by Carter Lee Aldridge (a found poem)

It seems to me I ought to write something
about or containing a reference to Lograire
—the mythical perfect kingdom of Lograire.
I'm going to complete my reading of Tolkien
books this year—like the Silmarillian.
It would have this line maybe:

'When I went walking in Lograire,
Who was there but Niameth, queen Niameth,
Who spoke, and said, "Drink, Issa Massi:
Deep red wine mixed with powder of roses.'
I've decided to name this kingdom we live in,
consisting of a broad mountain one mile high
and its slopes—Lograire..

We have a perfect roller-coaster road here,
like one I saw in Pennsylvania when I was a child
in my dad's car. It is a straight line, and it has
high peak curves and smaller dwindling curves.
[Carter drew a line approximating several small hills
with a couple of higher ones at the middle.] It's a joy
to see it (Jones Shaw Road and Cherokee Road).
Brevity is the soul of wit; communique ended.
May the Spirit of Perfection be with you.

PART TWO

Found Poems

THE FOLLOWING POEMS ARE drawn from the correspondence between Carter and myself that took place from the 1970's nearly until his death in 1990. They are created using the "found poem" or "erasure" technique, where words are cut away from prose to reveal a poem. Some words may be rearranged, but none are added. Except as otherwise noted, all are by Carter.

A SIMPLE LIFE

Well, I have been leading a relatively simple life lately,
or hope to if I am not. I rejoice over little things
as if they were not so little—like a cup of coffee
in the morning—or going to work at night.
I would like to celebrate everyday life more and more
—the routine that seems objectively dull but yields interior harmony. It is
what the world consists of—this exterior grind
of day to day work and routine. Floors need swept, furniture needs dusted,
dishes need done, and there are gardens to tend.
In the evening one's head nods to sleep while watching T.V.,
and so another day closes. There is so much
that we can do that we must be sure we are not greedy,
because we can't have or do it all. Someone somewhere says
it takes bravery to realize all that you will never experience.

It's true—experiences, careers and pleasures or pastimes
are all subdivided among us. We exchange some
of the experience by sharing, but a lot remains private,
enjoyed in a hidden state. So it goes—
we are mysteries to each other—because
self-knowledge is not easy to give to others.

PSALMS AND PROVERBS

Is there a psalm that goes like this?—

> From out of the pit,
> Yea, *even* from out of the pit,
> I called to Him,
> And he heard my cry.
> In an acceptable time
> I will call out to the Lord
> And he will bear me up.

Actually, this is the way I think of psalms in general
when I think of their general qualities.

Many times, alone, unable to bear a trouble any longer,
I have recited this psalm in prayer.

If the Lord gave me any objective answer in a voice
I think I would surely die of fright—it's not that

I'm looking for. I just want to pray and let my heart
be eased in prayer, when I use this psalmody.

You should check out the proverbs of Sirach sometime.
I think you know where to shop for a Catholic Bible.

I use the New American version (not the same as
The New American Standard).

> Joy is an excess of wisdom pouring over.

> Gratitude overcomes misery.

> A secret kept is tension on the bow.

Those are sayings I made up.

PSALM POEMS

by Matthew Robb Brown

I had written the following in a letter to Carter: "I am currently working on a collection [in] the style of the Psalms. These are coming to me fast and furious, in a way that [might suggest more] than simple poem-making [and] in some sense [could], when finished, bear a word from God as well as beauty. Normally I write in [an] earthy way, using imagery rather than direct statement, and while I believe this a sound way to make poems, I have had to depart from it due to the demands of the collection. I have enclosed the two pieces that are finished, 'Psalm of Waters' and 'Psalm of Man,' for you." ("One" here, I had titled "Psalm of Waters," followed by "Two," "Psalm of the Dove." I have not found "Psalm of Man" or any others.)—Matthew

One

Praise the Lord, all His people,
His heritage on earth;
Give the glory due His name.

The Lord gathers the waters,
He gathers them up from the sea.
He lifts them from the waves of Superior.

The grasses gladly spin mist
From their tips. The trees give easily
Off the pores of their leaves.

Lilac and rose in their season give it
With fragrance and lifted limb.
The Lord builds up His clouds—

Mighty heaps, castles, domes, anvils;
He stirs the wood like a pot
With His winds; then His rage

And cheer come down in strokes;
The Lord casts back, casts back His floods
On land and sea.

He soaks the furrow, fills the pond,
Laces the lake with whipped, woven lashes
And in a frenzy of laughter and joy

Dumps rain on the just and the unjust;
Gives man his crops,
Sets His bow in the clouds,

Locks them with hasps of color, His promise.
The Lord is faithful and true,
Full of compassion.

Trust in Him, sons of men, love Him,
and give Him your praise. Cast your hearts
At His feet in a joyful rain.

Two

When I wake to the laughter of poplar
And multitudes of birds,
And see the sunlight splash

Over the outer leaves,
With shadow behind,
Then I bless You.

On a street so quiet
I startled a mourning dove
To the gable, I cry out to You,

"Oh let me not startle Your Dove,
But let Him play
And let Him work where I live."

ON THE COMPANIONSHIP OF WOMEN

I'm into Bible-reading now, and I have certain
sadly unresolved hopes for the future of becoming
a priest. Yes, that's right. But as I say, my hopes
are unresolved—there's no focus on them. I figure,
well, I've made it alone so far, why not try
the complete route alone. There is a sort of aesthetic
appeal in repairing to our solitude, such as when
we hike through the woods.

I still think a lot of devotion to Mary, the mother
of Jesus. It strikes me that the image of the ideal
woman or eternal mother is helpful to someone
praying. It gives a sense of respect for women,
so I do pray that way.

I'm thinking of reading Dr. Zhivago again, and in
that very fine book Lara is a powerful symbol
that is obscurely related for me to the Blessed Virgin.

I was dating Mary Elizabeth Sullivan for at least
one year, and she was a schizophrenic mental patient
—I'm manic depressive, with schizo effect. We fell in
love and were considering marriage for the summer
of this year. Then came the news that she had a heart
condition and they wanted to operate. She died
on the operating table at the age of 46. Everybody said
she and I were suited for one another. I loved Mary
Elizabeth—she was very childlike, very dependent
upon the Lord. It took me nearly six years to find Mary.
How long will it take me to find another girlfriend?

INSCAPING

I bought a Keith Jarrett album (in a classical vein)
called In the Light. It features a string quartet which
I think is very good, as well as a brass quintet.
And lastly I found a good string quartet in Brahms'
String Quartet no. 3.

Also I'm reading some good books—some Freud,
Brothers Karamazov, a book on Spiritual Healing,
the poetry of Archibald MacLeish and of G.M.
Hopkins, and a book on Rational-Emotive therapy.
(It seems I still *do* get into poetry, after all).

I'm learning to relax more—in fact I believe
the Lord conveyed to me that I should slow down,
and that means in spending money too. So I am
slowing down in everything I need to do and
discovering that it relaxes me.

On one of those spring-like days we had recently,
when the snow was melting in the park (a block
away from here) I decided just to take a walk
to enjoy the out-of-doors. I found myself doing
some good inscaping (such as G.M. Hopkins did)
of the melting snow on the grass, the running water
and the quiet pools, and the sun in the trees. It gave me
a feeling I had really communed with nature. I think
inscaping is a direct non-verbal intuitive sensing of
beauty in the forms of nature. I especially love the pools
of water found in early spring. In Japan people control
their inscaping by making formal gardens, with stone
(and carved stones too), gravel, shaped trees, and running
water with perhaps bamboo tubes to convey

the water in places. I have a book which illustrates
this idea. I think the dictionary should carry a definition
of inscaping, but I don't think any do. It seems to me
to be a well- established word, wouldn't you say so?

ONE NIGHT IN AUTUMN

One night in autumn, while I was sitting drinking coffee
and reading Revelation in an all-night cafe,
the coffee cups, overturned on the racks, began to ring.
They rang for over five minutes while I read.
I didn't discontinue to take note of them.

Nobody seems to be making remarks about it,
but there were at least ten people there to witness.
I have concluded that for reasons of his own,
the Lord did a miracle.

One night in Lansing, Michigan I stood in the backyard
of a Roosevelt St. house and pointed my chrome-plated
utility knife at the sky for no particular reason and slashed
—and a brightly burning meteor fell that instant
in the same direction. So I tried again
and got the same result.

Weeks later at night in a schoolyard in Midland
I did the same thing and got the same result:
the immediate same direction fall of a meteor.
Since then I am loathe to try it anymore,
as I might be distracted if it happened too much.

Several articles, namely, nail-file/clipper sets, two,
and a key-chain tool set, one, were found by me
to be gold-plated in the last year. But I am sure
my family and I never bought such gold-plated items.
I took one to a pawn shop to confirm it being gold-plated,
I was so astonished. We had the articles all along,
it's just that they were not heretofore gold-plated.
I know we don't buy such items. Maybe the Lord
was trying to show his pleasure in my keeping of
and tending to an altar or private shrine in my
apartment. I didn't use to do that in Michigan.

SOMETIMES THOUGH

Sometimes though I like to write
a poem just for a friend, and I keep
no copy. I can't claim that this one
is that good, but it expresses a problem
I'm concerned with. "Greed is a form
of idol worship," the scripture says.
Sometimes I have conscientiously tried
to reduce my avarice for books, such as
this summer, but I still have trouble.
Such grandiose praises as are on book
covers are good for excitement, anyway,
and contribute to the general ferment.
I hope civilization lasts, and this poem
is about this. Your friend, Carter

There's an idol in the woods;
Its flank was gilded with natural herb
Colors, and its front bore expressions
Of meanness, stacked one on the other.
The *artist*, it was said, was no priest of
Orders, but only a common man
In search of hidden form.
His waist deep in water,
He forded the mountain stream,
Clinging to a rope. Who's to judge,
Then, the quality imbued when form
Is invested in a thing so common,
Yet divine, as being
Ourselves made abstract
So as to last? It was dead, and only
The attention lavished on it
Could determine the matter.
The enmity gone, we had
High art and civilization.

WORKING

I'm writing in my living room at around
noontime. I've been working steadily as a
security guard, and I've met some new people
who are rather nice or interesting. Sometimes
I feel inferior to those with more lucrative or more
demanding types of jobs. What I do is so simple . . .
But I suppose there is integrity even in my job. I
have experienced more stability as a result of
working, because I am so thankful for the leisure
time I do have that my leisure is more rewarding.

Sometimes I think I could affirm and attest
that man is fallen, because I sense an ideal
harmony that I cannot reach, an interpersonal
harmony. A song—But I see life rough and haggard—
or as one writer said, life is nasty, brutish, and short.

I was happy yesterday to have found some nice
clothes used and on sale—I picked up two sports
jackets—for $3.00 and $1.00. Clothes seem to mean
a lot to my personal well-being in society—I like
to sport flashy stuff, sometimes as a sort of joke.

When I awoke today the thought was coming to my
mind that priests are poets—after all, they glorify
water and wine in front of a lot of people, and who
would do a thing like that except a poet? A hired
poet, one who celebrates life for and with and
in front of others. It's just a thought.

I hope you are enjoying 'the green clasp of summer,
wherein one's heart is entwined.' Your friend, Carter

TOMORROW I HAVE HIGH HOPES

I'm on watch now, listening to my radio
in the guard shack. I was not able to find
the book of poetry you sent me, but that is
only temporary. I read some of the poems
in it and was favorable to them. I was involved
in reading my book of Emily Dickinson's poems
the other day and they aroused in me some
degree of new ardor, inspired me to write some
poems myself. I find the rewards of writing
poetry to be delicate and meager in oneself,
but the rewards of reading it and believing in it
to an extent to be copious. I can also believe in
the person behind the poetry, such as the Emily
Dickinson whom I admire and respect in the
breathless grandeur of some of her lines. I was
only turned on quite as much to the poetry
of W.B. Yeats, recently.

Tomorrow I have high hopes of doing some
more painting of our house for my mother. I want
so to do a good job but pulling me down in hopes
is the fact that some parts of that house are decaying
and I can't do a thing about it. Fortunately, they are few.
I went on a flurry of buying for it—DeRusto rust-
preventative paint and some spackling paste for cracks,
although I don't know if our ladder or its lack of stability
will allow me to reach all the cracks. But as I say, I have
poured some hopes into the task and I feel motivated
to do a good job. If my attitude were that it's busywork
or slaving I wouldn't be able to work at it with as much satisfaction, so I try
to reform my attitude somewhat
and then its pleasant aspects appear.

I dug up some grown potatoes two days ago—they were small but I'm glad they appeared. There are probably more, but I haven't dug for them yet.

I ASK MYSELF

How does one proclaim God's mercy to others,
I ask myself . . .

The amen in a church (like our Catholic church
here) at communion seems to say "So be it" to his
death on the cross, but isn't it to say "yes, confirm
me in the word; I believe"? I've often wondered,
and pictured the priest as a judge, who even goes
so far as to imitate Pilate's washing his hands
of the death of Jesus. In fact the Catholic priest
re-enacts much of what happened in the Bible,
but in a symbolic form. Really communion is
meant to be a celebration, like a fellowship meal.

Thank you for your letter, Matthew. I read it
again today. I consider you very childlike to be able
to speak at all of the devil, more childlike than myself.
The deville [sic] is no harbinger, he is an old haranguer
from way back. In the Bible it states: "Be children in
malice, and in mind mature." It's true, however, that
some corrupt pornographic literature I've had has
affected me adversely in my spirit; it's very existence
irritated me (of course, I gave into it, you know *that*,
Matthew). I think that pornography is an abuse of
photographic power to stop someone in motion. A real
woman is much more slippery and elusive; a man
desires to pin her down, in a sense, or wants to
corral or corner her.

I think you are brave to do some of the things you do. I know there are certain traditions of which we are a part, such as J.R.R. Tolkien, Charles Williams, and C.S. Lewis. I can sense that we are part of such popular writings as these. Some of my writings are *serendipity* writings—they delight in discovery by accident.

ON TEMPTATIONS, TRIALS, AND VICES

Sometimes I believe I have been tempted
by some foreign agency of disaster or mistrust.
Calling it, as you do, the devil, just won't come
to my lips, and I retain an old discretion against
such talk. But what of this summer, when I lost
some finely constructed writing to a strange
impulse to destroy it? (I set writings aflame).
That I know I cannot explain.

I believe in stripping naked before a woman, as
a part of preparation for marriage—I believe the
man should at least view his woman naked, and her
him, too—and I feel this way because I believe that
as the "two shall become one flesh," they should
have their eyesight filled with each other.

I joined the choir of St. Brigid's but I missed the
last mass in which they sang, unfortunately. The
young adults club of Midland is going to go up to
Sanford Lake soon to spend the day there. I am
looking forward to that, because the last excursion
was a joy to me. I had a wonderful time there on
the beach with all that water around. I felt somewhat
playful and the water seemed somewhat sexual to me,
curiously enough. I got up on water skis once but fell
down the other times.

I've taken up pipe smoking—I still smoke cigarettes
too. I don't believe it causes cancer and I believe it is
a divine art. "For every unworthy smoke, a choke." I
look like I'm 30 by the way, not 40—I simply haven't
shown aging as much as some people.

My fig tree is bearing ripe figs right now. I'd like to
trim it so that it will bear more next year. It is only
about 12 feet high more or less.
It was getting awful hectic up there in Smyrna
and Marietta. Psychic communication had become
a terrible problem for me.

When it is amicable, warm and humorous, psychic
communication turns into one of the desiderata,
but not so when it enters conflict and mental war
of group on group or region on region.

Yet there was bound to be some Christian conflict or
in other words war to settle some issues—like certain
people saying I don't have sufficient I.Q. to be a
linoleum-block artist. That is a fascist lie. And the aim
and intent is to repress my *real* intelligence—as apart
from my paper intelligence.

Besides, I know that my spirit is extremely intelligent
—I mean apart from my mind.

I haven't had a drink of alcoholic beverage in at least
20 months—and I intend to make that permanent with
the exception of communion wine, whenever I encounter
it again in a state of grace.

My reading of Scripture is regular—not completely
regular, but improved over what it would be if I let
the devil distract me from its daily use, as once he
seemed able to do. I use the King James version 80%
of the time, now. Some missing reform is going on:
about resentments, when to & when not to show anger
or frustration to others, or when to forbear in the Lord's
name; and smoking: it is 80% reduced in my life and
with grace's influence now having come, the desire to
smoke is fading fast, like smoke.

By keeping busy with intelligent use of time, and by a resolution to take care of, with self-respect, the body I have been given to use, I have won a moral victory over my weak-kneed attitudes about smoking that preceded. I now see how, with grace, I can reject smoking, and repent in a positive direction. Pray for all of us, that we will be able to support ourselves as a family as soon as we need to, and not on welfare, I hope.

Thank you, Matthew, for just being there as a consciousness on the other end of this letter. In Christ's Love,
—Carter

GEORGIA

I would rather not describe Georgia as it is
now—it would be too premature. We're having
fair weather right now, cold only at night. The
house and the lot are nice; the backyard goes
back 75 yards or so to a stream. The garden can
be watered from the stream with a portable pump.
The soil here is almost universally of a reddish tint.
There is a preponderance of pine trees in all woody
areas, unless they've been deliberately altered.
My mother can grow both a summer and winter
garden—her winter garden has been planted these
two weeks running.

I hang out at a friendly pub and restaurant 1 block
away, named Howard's; there one can share beer,
T.V. (Monday or Sunday football, etc.), and friendly
conversation at the bar. Or, get inexpensive heavily
stacked sandwiches—their specialty—and pizza too.
People seem to know each other there, being
Marietta/Smyrna locals.

GRANDEUR

I was recently reading *Seven Storey Mountain*
by Thomas Merton and it was filled with
august sadness; a serenity or worshipful coloration
pervaded it. I fell in love with it, since it has a
powerful faith expressed in it, in very direct terms.
Thomas Merton really got into Catholicism, it seems
—and he made a commitment to it that lasted
through the years.

It's so true—God's grandeur is in the world.
Men have seen it and yet not acted upon what they saw.
It's strange, isn't it, to go unmoved by the beauty that
is all around us, nurturing us and inflaming us by turns?
For instance the farms all planted out, and the blue flowers
that now line the roads; crowds walking downtown
—the bustle that ambition brings. These things are often
good to see for me.

I do enjoy these days at home. The radio plays,
the T.V. blares, the record machine whirls its songs
with a singular elan and all in all there is a variety to life
that can fill me up to brimming with mental activity.
It's then that I feel most the need for discipline
and for cutting down on input. Blessings
—Your Friend, Carter

Do read "Ecclesiastes," or The Preacher, in the Bible,
if you want a sense of how the Lord condones ongoing
labors in and for themselves, or for the pleasure thereof.
Margery Roberts, a teacher of mine, once spoke to me
of how wonderful it is that we are filled to overflowing
with enough work to keep us busy, so that we don't
have to be continually dwelling on the past.

ARTISTS AND THEIR DISCONTENT

It will be all right if you publish the poem
you found in my letters, but please don't use
my name in connection with it. I started working
as an artist again this winter after I had quit for
ten months or so. This work enclosed is not quite
all of my work since then. Art is a lovely game
indeed. By failing to print many of certain prints
before altering the design or destroying the original,
I make rare objects. I have several rare prints now
of unusual quality. But this art thing is strictly like
working with the earth—I do it as an everyday
chore. I am so shy of overglorifying a work of art
and so killing its raison d'etre.

I no longer read poetry at all, and I fail to understand
it when I do. But it does seem a bit vain to assume
on high that (I) (we) (YOU) can speak the English
language better than most others, and then to flaunt
it in their face. I think most book writing for literary
purposes stinks of vanity. Some books escape this
holy fire of mine, but I won't look for them anymore.
'Vanity of vanity, all is vanity.'

I think the poem you wanted me to O.K. has a nice
ending. It really affected me strongly after I first read
it. I even thought it sounded to me like a gesture of
defiance to the world, a mild one. I don't know why
it affected me that way.

I would like your reaction to these art works. If you
want to give any to someone else, that's O.K. I think
that having not worked as an artist for ten months
produced a surprise. Bon jour. Carter

DESIRE FOR LEARNING AND THE LOVE OF GOD

I sit here in Camp Burns, outside of the main part
of Little Rock, Arkansas—and sounds of night
—rich sounds of locusts, or whatever they are—
thick sounds—surround me, seem to want to close
in around me . . . they are very close to me, and night
hovers all around this little battery-lamp at the table,
seeming to witness to my letter, almost—Nature,
here, is very rich, a Presence cultured deeply by
warmth of the South . . .

It is very warm, and morning hours of six AM
will be the coolest (in the low 70's at most). My
Mother, and Bruce, are sleeping in the tent, and
I will too, soon—depending upon how late I
choose to stay awake, reading poetry, or a Bible,
or my journal . . . My journal has been as an
intimate companion, to me, made more so
because, in every one of them (they are all *one*
running account, since I keep dates on entries)
there is some witness of Jesus, who keeps me from
falling, despite the intense allurement of many,
possibly lurid, desires . . . Again, though I *knew* I
was on the brink of even *desiring* sins of pleasure
and self-indulgence of various sorts—whether it
be drink, smoking, or sexual adventuresome-ness,
I have opened it, in honesty, to Jesus . . . I *know* that
I am vile, that the desires are there. I *tell* this to my
Lord, and He knows—He understands . . . He knows
what I really am, because I confess it to Him—
and I am lifted, because He is here. My imaginations
want to carry me into lurid excesses, but my *fate*
demands that I see that now, and inevitably later too,
I must be alone with Him—Jesus . . . And so I wax

content again, but keep enough of *motivation* in the
"Desire for Learning"—as the first words of a book
I own reads—(I *think* its title is *The Desire For
Learning and God*) Hasn't it always been true for us
two, and P.J.S. equally, that our "Desire for Learning
and God" has kept us busy in those moments when we
faced our temptations? Now I remember—here is the
book's title, corrected: *"The Desire for Learning and
the Love of God,"* by Dom Lequerq—a study of
monastic scholarship and arts in the centuries of
monastic leadership in schooling—Though I've only
read a little of it, the title seemed of a singular purity
to me, as one who studies books . . . and as one who
loves the Lord, as he *must*—for, to me, to love the
Lord is something *always* made urgent by outside
pressures upon me—as if, to make a metaphor, the
calamitous outside pressure of the world would collapse
me, did I not contrive a way, through prayer, to oppose
to it an *equal* pressure from the *inside* . . . Perhaps, had
my desires not been as constantly frustrated, in my life, as
they have been, I would have not come *flying* into the
Lord's arms with such eager devotion, as I now do so
(for I *must*).

Perhaps, then, I would have had a fillip of hope *left* in
those desires, and so, not have wished for the life of
meditative prayer, recollection, and indeed—shall I say it
—*priesthood*—as much as I have wished for it. *Often*, even
on this trip, I have gotten high on my desire to be, in
some sense, one more *good* priest for the Lord—loving
humanity from its grey shades of mundaneness, right
through its *infrequent* flashes of *real* glory—I mean, its
true-gold-moments, rather than its pyrites . . . I often
contemplate on the *inward* beauty of humanity,
behind its *outward* coat, which remains, for me,
monotonous grey . . . Outwardly, take humanity of *all* ages,
and the outward color of outwardly seen humanity is—
simply grey . . . Youth flashes other colors, in hope—but in the
aged, the forlorn, the drudges, we see a better wisdom

growing inwardly beautiful, and we see the aged calm
our (youth's) flashy surfaces and pride of life with *their*
humble grey. I love the aged people I meet . . . They have
not that delusive finery of appearance that we could
wish for (seeing it much), so we are *content* to wish for
their inward beauties—which, however frail of limb they
may be—are ruddy, hale, and strong beauties indeed—
inculcations of all life's outward perceptions, now distilled,
sifted down to Fact . . . not illusion . . . One glory of youth,
fit to be wrestled down, in rebellion, to the yokes this life
puts on them—and one glory of the aged: that they express
a lifetime of emotional weathers well-weathered . . . And
some acceptance of commitment, a hard yoke, but one
leading to life . . . I still love Robert Frost's saying, found
in his recorded sayings or writings somewhere (there's a
lot of it, if you look . . .)—"Freedom is working easy in
harness." Biblical, it is, too—just compare, for origins,
"My burden is light, my yoke is sweet . . ."

When I recall the anecdote about Joseph Conrad, novelist,
who once, at a pub, in realizing, as he sat there, a whole
plan for a new novel—began to cry, knowing the hard
disciplined duty before him, of writing it—*then* I know
writers who submit themselves to be obedient to God
have a cross to bear in their writer's tasks . . . Now, please
pray for me, us, Mom, Bruce, and I—that God's mercy
see us safely home . . . Please say a kind prayer . . .—Carter

FEBRUARY 19, 1979

I hope your address is still the same, as I write this.
How were your house-heating costs this winter
so far, as a comparison to recent years? I'd be curious
to know how Michiganders fare with respect to rising
energy costs and more severe winters . . . I suppose,
though, it doesn't go as hard on community-houses
where most or all are wage-earners—which makes a
good argument for the reliability of the Christian plan
of more intimate and close-numbered sharing of
quarters and food, a plan made psychologically
practicable by adoption of Christian ethos, and
impractical, it would seem to me, by a thorough
rejection of the more profound religious ramifications
of "sharing all things alike" that goes counter to a
typical capitalist rage for hoarding of the most space,
the most privacy, the most goods per each individual
as possibly might be. When does the act of ordering
all things around increased individual space and privacy
reach an extent in which privacy become selfishness,
and worse, even a kind of narcissism? So, Matthew,
if you now live in a "community-house" or similar
concept, I believe that you are directly studying a
phenomenon of life which for better or for worse is
radically relevant to Christianity itself—so do study
it well. I guess you might call this "exhortation."
I hope that it wasn't totally uncalled for, in your situation.

I would love to hear from you, and see some of your writings—but please don't make the mistake of interrupting some spiritual/literary growth at a time when talking of, or exposing it, would place hindrance to graces more important in that they are carrying you closer to God, and not nearly so important for purposes of my paltry observance of them. Deo Gratias, Sincerely, Carter

LATE IN 1978

by Matthew Robb Brown

Ted Reid, my pastor, took me to Severence Tool
Industries, a company where he worked before he
went into the ministry full time. I had an interview,
and was hired to work in their machine grind
department. So I bade Begick's Nursery a fond
farewell. I'm working the night shift. It's quite
exacting work, because you have to grind a tool
to a specification within so many thousandths of
an inch. But I'm learning how true it is that "I can
do all things through Christ who strengthens me."
It's good work and in a Christian atmosphere
because many Christians run it and work there.

I've been doing more poetry lately than I have
since I moved here.

Your sheet of poetry arrived here a few days after
your letter, I believe it was the day after my reply
went out, so that's why I never commented on them.
To tell you the unvarnished truth, I think they have
possibilities but lack finish and direction. The best
one is "how the glory hurts &c." "Having Driven to
Hill Church" has stimulating images, especially in
the second half. Some of the language seems stiff or,
at least, affected, but that poem is worth working on.
The last line stands out to me as a good line.
"Quiet Time"—I'm not sure where this one is coming
from or going. Is it based on some legend? Again,
"Out in the garden . . ." is the best. It has an endearingly
classic feel about it.

I've started shooting pictures (b&w) of the old
architecture around Bay City and hope to do more,
especially when the weather improves, though if I
have the gumption, there are good winter effects
to be captured.

We've had quite a few small snow storms, nothing
major yet. I bet it'll be weird not having snow for
Christmas, for you, but when January comes I'll
envy you.

LETTER TO CARTER, IN MY YOUTH

by Matthew Robb Brown

I think of and pray for you often. I know He
loves you deeply. We must learn continually
to quell the rhythm of our own minds and attain
to catch that Song our loving Father is ever singing.
It is the song of creation, and He sings it in and among
His redeemed people as He constantly creates them.
His image may grow sharper in us daily if we thus
cooperate. To think God's thoughts after Him
—this is far removed from every kind of "groupthink"
and thought formula. The more we are in God's image,
the less we are like each other, but the more interlocked
and interdependent we become, like the diversifying
organ systems in a developing child. All things are done
in Jesus and in love. He is the great King and my
strong tower. Forgive me for being a bit rambling,
but I love to think about my Lord, and this letter
affords a place where we can share those thoughts.

APRIL 9, 1987

Dear Mat[thew] and Kay,

I am in the hospital temporarily, and I decided
to send you the sketch on the other side. I hope
you enjoy this piece of art nouveau. If you put it
under some books it will flatten out. Time moves
slowly here. We play bingo several nights a week
for free money donated by various veterans' groups
in the area. So far I have won $10.

I still keep a shrine of sorts at home, and in the
summer it will have fruits and flowers on it, and
an oil wick lamp. It is very symbolic, and it puts
my mind at rest to have it in my room.

I'm going to have a show of my prints in the V.A.
Hospital library in September. I copied my
"Poems for B. Lee" and gave them to a couple of
people. They like them—but handing out copies is
all I plan to do in the way of publication. I also hand
out copies of "Poem for Kildarrow" and "Sirenon's
Praise."

I drive a '71 Plymouth Duster that I got for $375.
I have put about $500.00 into it in various repairs
and new tires. My mother is unemployed because
of her arthritic hands, so my younger brother and I
support her and keep a hold on the property, which
we plan to someday own outright. There is a flowing
streamlet in back of the back yard.

I am dating Mary Sullivan and she wants to marry me.
She is in her 40's like me and has never married or had
any children. Remember the brotherhood, Mat[thew].
Sincerely yours, Carter Lee Aldridge

Appendix

MATTHEW ROBB BROWN'S POEMS about Carter or which were discussed in our conversation or correspondence.

DELICATE LIGHT

by Matthew Robb Brown

Delicate light
laps into foliaged forest,
dousing the floor
with statements of oak,
sighs of cedar,
liquid, interior,
substanceless, powerful,
insinuating the scene
like plants through pavement
sprouted from seeds of night
touching pollen of
delicate light.
(written in notebook at Green Lake,
Wisconsin, July 1974)

DOMES

by Matthew

A recollection

As we walked together
along East Saint Andrew
Avenue, Carter and I, beside
Barstow Woods, he was
telling me the story
of a ruin he went through
once, a house of domes
begun, never finished,
because a rich man had
become poor. It was a set
of sturdy egg shells with an
atrium, on prime wooded land
in Michigan, where birds
circled the glassless light,
chipmunks scurried
through acorns on the floors,
and your voice could really
echo in the empty domes
of that magnificent home.

BIRCHES

by Matthew Robb Brown

Birches, straight and slanted,
bowed and rigid, support each other
in march across the rise and hollow
of sand, lichen, loam.

In stillness poised for a sound,
they show a slow cellmasonry of growth:
Increments of wood
burst taut bands like Lazarus.
Wind papers them across the forest like guidons.

Choose a home, a cottage,
in the forest baseland, with knarry wood
walls, clocks carved to time tunes;
books to line the halls and windows to frame the land.

In full time he comes riding his birch-hued horse,
lifting me up behind him,
riding off in the fury of wind;
dropping our winding-sheets behind.

(Carter once said that this poem gave him an aesthetic experience
while he was babysitting in a house that featured a lot of good woodwork. It
was published in the Autumn 1975 issue of *Green River Review,* which also
contained two poems translated from the Spanish by Carter, the original
versions of which came from Luisa Pasamanik.)

TWO POEMS

by Luisa Pasamanik

Carter Lee Aldridge, translator.

These translations by Carter appeared in the Fall 1975 issue of *Green River Review*, along with my poem "Birches" above. They were printed facing the Spanish texts, which are not included here because of copyright considerations.

ANGEL

I call you angel.

Always angel.

Although you wound or kill,
although you forbid.

Angel.

I call you angel.

Although you make use of
all that
hurts and bleeds.

Angel.

I call you angel.

Always angel.

By myself, sad, fleeing,
I call you angel.
Fear is a specter.
We invent it.

In the air
every day
we invent it.

And fear grows.

It courses
through my blood,
through your blood.

Fear tempts.

It says:
kill,
die.

It forces
me to lose you,
and you to lose me.

But I call you angel.

Brother,
brother angel.

Here, amidst darkness.

Call me too.

XX

HOLD your sigh.

All that is in the air
and in the earth
flowers.

Flowers and trembles.

I await you
behind
my skin,
behind
my voice,
behind
all limits,
in back of
all fear,
in back of
all doubt,
or former shadow.

I want to be you
in perpetual circling.

And I want you to be in me.

We will travel the earth,
all the earth
in order to rescue the light.
And then,
angels,
angels, after all,
we will go
to build liberty.

MORE THAN I COULD ASK OR THINK

by Matthew R. Brown.

We used to argue back and forth, my friend;
Your education steeped in Freud and Jung,
And my baptised-behind-the-ears new faith.
And I would warn that Jesus soon will come
To call His people on, to Heaven's pier,
While you'd protest that this earth has its joys
You wouldn't want to leave, for something strange.

I poured my tears to God for you in prayer,
And in my struggle nearly felt despair
Because it seemed as if your coming home
Depended all upon my efforts there.

I fell asleep, and I began to dream,
And felt as though I stood before the Throne
Where God the Father sits, with Christ beside.
And there you stood beside me, and the joy
I felt at that could barely be contained.
Before the Father we embraced, my friend.

These are the words you later wrote to me:
"We should prepare ourselves to meet the Lord.
This is our hope, this is our heritage.
We will meet Him someday, and we will see:
He will be beautiful; He will be beautiful."

Written January 1992 according to the typescript. This recounts a dream, which I can recall vividly, that occurred in 1973. It also contains biographical / historical information that should be included here. I don't claim for it any literary value beyond its relevance to the present book, the best part of it being what Carter wrote.

LETTERS FROM A FRIEND, 1974

(a poem "found" in letters of Carter Aldridge. The material used for this older erasure poem appears in different form in the erasures above.—MRB.)

1
I do enjoy these days at home.
The radio plays, the t.v. blares,
the record machine whirls its songs
with a singular elan
and all in all there is a variety to life
that can fill me to brimming.

2
I hope you are enjoying "the green clasp
of summer, wherein one's heart is entwined."

3
I rejoice over little things
as if they were not little
—a cup of coffee in the morning;
going to work at night.
I would like to celebrate
everyday life more and more
—the routine that seems dull
but yields interior harmony.

4
There is much we can do; we must be sure
we are not greedy because we can't have or do it all.
Someone somewhere says it takes bravery
to realize all that you will never experience.

5
I consider you very childlike
to speak at all of the devil
—more childlike than myself.
The deville is no harbinger
—he is an old haranguer from way back.
"Be children in malice, in mind mature."

6
Sometimes I think I could affirm that man is fallen;
I sense an ideal I cannot reach, an interpersonal song
—but I see life rough, haggard or, as one writer said,
"nasty, brutish, and short."
God's grandeur is in the world.
It's strange, isn't it, to go unmoved by the beauty
that is all around us, nurturing
and inflaming us by turns:
the farms all planted out;
the blue flowers that now line the roads;
crowds walking downtown.
These are good to see.

7
The wind blows toward me;
leaning into it, I say,
"Stardrops in clusters,
raiments in wind;
rain on the dust,
and harmony in air."
For all these things so fair,
the things of pity
will grow strangely dear . . .

[This technique involves removing material from a found original [gener-
ally prose] until it emerges as a poem. One doesn't change any remaining
original words. The exception here is that section 7 is most of the original
words of a fragment of verse included in a letter and, as far as I know, no-
where else. Matthew]

Bibliography

Silva, Phil, Ed: *Your Own Poets*, an anthology of Christian poems, Midland, Michigan: Praise the Lord Press, 1977. pp. 16–21 by count. (The pages in this chapbook are not numbered.)

Tyner, Raymond, Ed: *Green River Review* Volume VI Number 3, Fall 1975. University Center, Michigan: The Green River Press, Inc. p. 15 and pp. 24–29.

Bibliographical Note: the issue of *Green River Review* noted above contains my poem, "Birches," as well as Carter's translations from the Spanish of two poems from Luisa Pasamanik's *The Exiled Angel* (Buenos Aires: Desterrado, 1962). I thought it best to retain the word "Press" in both of these references to make it clear that these are the names of the publishers.

www.ingramcontent.com/pod-product-compliance
Lightning Source LLC
Chambersburg PA
CBHW071139090426
42736CB00012B/2165